United States Government Accountability Office

Report to Congressional Requesters

December 2012

TAX GAP

IRS Could Significantly Increase Revenues by Better Targeting Enforcement Resources

GAO

Accountability ★ Integrity ★ Reliability

GAO-13-151

TAX GAP

IRS Could Significantly Increase Revenues by Better Targeting Enforcement Resources

Highlights of GAO-13-151, a report to congressional requesters

Why GAO Did This Study

Heightened attention to federal deficits has increased pressure on IRS to reduce the tax gap—the difference between taxes owed and taxes paid on time—and better enforce taxpayer compliance. Resource limitations and concern over taxpayer burden, however, prevent IRS from auditing more than a small fraction of individual income tax returns filed. How IRS allocates these limited resources demands careful consideration.

As requested, this report (1) describes how IRS allocates resources across individual taxpayer compliance enforcement programs and across types of taxpayers within each program; (2) estimates the direct revenue return on investment for the individual taxpayer enforcement programs and the extent of variation across those programs and across types of taxpayers; and (3) determines the potential for gains from shifting resources from lower-yielding programs and types of taxpayers to higher-yielding ones.

To accomplish these objectives GAO analyzed IRS data on 2007 and 2008 tax returns, reviewed IRS documentation, and interviewed appropriate IRS officials.

What GAO Recommends

GAO recommends that IRS review disparities in the ratios of direct revenue yield to costs across different enforcement programs and across different groups of cases and consider this evidence as a potential basis for adjusting its allocation of enforcement resources each year. IRS agreed with the recommendations.

View GAO-13-151. For more information, contact James White at (202) 512-9110 or whitej@gao.gov

What GAO Found

The Internal Revenue Service (IRS) spends most of its enforcement resources on examinations. Correspondence exams of individual tax returns, which target fewer and simpler compliance issues, are significantly less costly on average than the broader and more complex field exams. GAO estimated that the average cost (including overhead) of correspondence exams opened in 2007 and 2008 was $274, compared to an average of $2,278 for field exams. IRS spent almost 20 percent of the $1.6 billion per year that it devoted to exams on returns from taxpayers with positive income of at least $200,000, even though such returns accounted for only 3 percent of the 136 million individual returns filed per year. (Positive income, a measure that IRS uses to classify returns for exam planning purposes, disregards losses that may offset this income).

GAO estimated that, for the 2 years of cases reviewed, correspondence exams were significantly more productive in terms of direct revenue produced per dollar of cost than field exams. As shown in the figure below, both types of exams of taxpayers with positive incomes of at least $200,000 were significantly more productive than exams of lower-income taxpayers.

Direct Revenue Return on Investment for Different Types of Exams and Groups of Individual Income Tax Returns Opened in 2007 and 2008

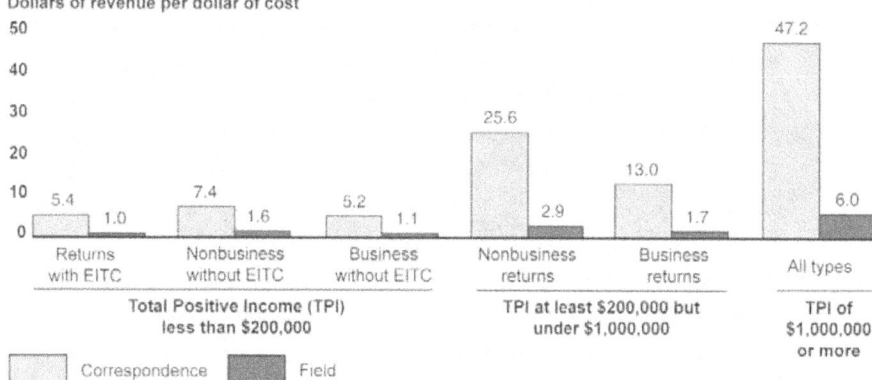

Source: GAO analysis of IRS data

Note: EITC is the earned income tax credit

GAO demonstrated how these estimates could be used to inform resource allocation decisions. For example, a hypothetical shift of a small share of resources (about $124 million) from exams of tax returns in less productive groups shown in the figure to exams in the more productive groups could have increased direct revenue by $1 billion over the $5.5 billion per year IRS actually collected (as long as the average ratio of direct revenue to cost for each category of returns did not change). These gains would recur annually, relative to the revenue that IRS would collect if it did not change its resource allocation. This particular resource shift would not reduce exam coverage rates significantly and, therefore, should have little, if any, negative effect on voluntary compliance.

_____ **United States Government Accountability Office**

Contents

Figures

Abbreviations

AIMS	Audit Information Management System
ASFR	Automated Substitute for Return
AUR	Automated Underreporter
EITC	earned income tax credit
ERIS	Enforcement Revenue Information System
IFS	Integrated Financial System
IRP	Information Returns Processing
IRS	Internal Revenue Service
NRP	National Research Program
SB/SE	Small Business/Self-Employed
W&I	Wage and Investment

United States Government Accountability Office
Washington, DC 20548

December 5, 2012

The Honorable Max Baucus
Chairman
The Honorable Orrin Hatch
Ranking Member
Committee on Finance
United States Senate

The Honorable Charles Grassley
Ranking Member
Committee on the Judiciary
United States Senate

Heightened attention to federal deficits has increased pressure on the Internal Revenue Service (IRS) to reduce the tax gap—the difference between taxes owed and taxes paid on time—and better enforce taxpayer compliance. Resource limitations and interest in minimizing taxpayer burden, however, prevent IRS from auditing anything but a small fraction of the total number of individual income tax returns filed for a given tax year. Of the approximately 141 million individual tax returns filed in 2010, only 1.1 percent were formally audited. IRS has developed several compliance enforcement programs with the goal of increasing taxpayer compliance, using resources more efficiently, and minimizing taxpayer burden. These programs, which include computer-based matching systems and streamlined correspondence audits (which do not involve face-to-face meetings with taxpayers) designed for less complex issues, fill different roles in the compliance enforcement strategy. Every year IRS publishes information regarding the coverage rates and additional taxes assessed through these various programs, but relatively little information is available on how much revenue is actually collected as a result of these enforcement activities (called direct revenue). Even less information is available regarding program performance with respect to identifiable subpopulations (varying in terms of income levels, and types of income) covered by the enforcement programs.

Given the importance of appropriately allocating limited resources, you asked us to assess the performance of IRS's enforcement programs. In this report we (1) describe how IRS allocates resources across individual taxpayer compliance enforcement programs and across types of taxpayers within each program; (2) estimate the direct revenue return on investment for the individual taxpayer compliance enforcement programs and the extent of variation across those programs and across types of taxpayers; and (3) determine the potential for gains from shifting resources from lower-yielding programs and types of taxpayers to higher-yielding ones.

To describe how IRS allocates resources across individual taxpayer compliance enforcement programs and across types of taxpayers within each program, we compared the amounts of resources that IRS devotes to each of four broad enforcement programs for individuals who file form 1040 tax returns—Automated Underreporter (AUR), Automated Substitute for Return (ASFR), correspondence examination, and field examination.[1] These programs are described below in the background section. We also report the cost of cases worked and the percentage of total returns covered by correspondence and field exam programs. For the correspondence and field exam programs, we make these comparisons across the principal groups of individual taxpayers (defined in terms of positive income size and characteristics of their returns, such as the presence of the earned income tax credit (EITC)) that IRS uses for exam planning purposes.[2] We use program cost data obtained from IRS's Integrated Financial System (IFS) and data on the number of cases from IRS's Enforcement Revenue Information System (ERIS). We also use data on coverage rates from IRS's Data Book.[3] Our analyses to support all three of our objectives cover enforcement cases opened in fiscal years 2007 and 2008 (the latest years of data available at the time of our analysis in which the large majority of cases have worked their way through the collection process).[4]

---

[1]We exclude the Math Error program from our detailed review because it covers 100 percent of tax returns filed and, therefore, does not involve the same types of resource allocation decisions that are relevant to the other programs.

[2]In general, total positive income is the sum of all positive amounts shown for the various sources of income reported on the individual tax return and, thus, excludes losses.

[3]Internal Revenue Service, Data Book, 2009, Publication 55B, Washington, DC, March 2010, and Data Book, 2008, March 2009.

[4]Although IRS typically reports enforcement data according to the fiscal year in which cases are closed, we report our results according to the fiscal year in which the cases were opened because that better reflects the populations of cases that IRS targeted in their annual exam planning process.

To estimate the direct revenue return on investment for the individual taxpayer compliance enforcement programs, we obtained data from ERIS on collections of tax, interest, and penalties directly attributable to specific types of exams for different groups of taxpayers, as well as those attributable to AUR and ASFR cases. We also obtained cost data from IFS for these four programs. For the field exam program, available data allow us to incorporate differences in the length, difficulty, and location of audits into our cost comparisons. Our return on investment measure is computed as the ratio of revenues over costs with the value of the revenues discounted for any delays between the year in which IRS expended the money on the enforcement cases and the year in which the revenues were collected.

To determine the potential for gains from shifting resources from lower-yielding programs and types of taxpayers to higher-yielding ones, we use our results from the second objective to demonstrate how modest reallocations of resources would affect total collections, assuming that additional cases examined in a particular group would be approximately as productive as the average case in that group. We also interviewed IRS officials and reviewed the technical literature on tax enforcement to identify factors beyond the direct revenue return on investment that IRS should consider when making adjustments to its resource allocations.

We determined for the purposes of this review that the data used were reliable. (See app. I for additional information about our methodology.) We conducted this performance audit from November 2009 through December 2012 in accordance with generally accepted government auditing standards. Those standards require that we plan and perform the audit to obtain sufficient, appropriate evidence to provide a reasonable basis for our findings and conclusions based on our audit objectives. We believe that the evidence obtained provides a reasonable basis for our findings and conclusions based on our audit objectives.

Background

In January 2012, IRS estimated that the gross tax gap—the difference between taxes owed and taxes paid on time—was $450 billion in tax year 2006. IRS estimated that it would eventually recover about $65 billion of this amount through late payments and enforcement actions, leaving a net tax gap of $385 billion. The tax gap has been a persistent problem in spite of extensive congressional and IRS efforts to reduce it. In past work we have said that reducing the tax gap will not likely be achieved through a single solution. Rather, the tax gap must be attacked on multiple fronts and with multiple strategies over a sustained period of time. On the enforcement front, IRS's efforts to ensure compliance of individual taxpayers combine several distinct programs that collectively monitor and correct noncompliance with income tax filing, reporting, and payment requirements. These programs fill different roles in the enforcement process and vary in the number of taxpayers covered, the resources used, and their level of automation.

Math Error Program:

IRS's Math Error program electronically checks all filed tax returns for obvious math errors as returns are processed. The Math Error program reviews and adjusts items specifically listed in Internal Revenue Code section 6213. The specific issues that the program has authority to review include calculation errors, entries that are inconsistent with or exceed statutory limits, various omissions, inclusions, and entries of information, or incorrect use of an IRS table.

Automated Underreporter Program:

IRS collects information on taxpayers from employers, financial institutions, and other third parties and compiles these data in the Information Returns Processing (IRP) system. The Automated Underreporter (AUR) program electronically matches the IRP data against the information that taxpayers report on their forms 1040 as a means of identifying potentially underreported income or unwarranted deductions or tax credits. The matching process takes place months after taxpayers have filed their tax returns. For tax year 2010, AUR identified approximately 23.8 million potential discrepancies between taxpayer income, deduction, and other information reported by third parties and the information supplied by taxpayers on their individual income tax returns. IRS officials said that resource constraints prevent them from contacting taxpayers for all of the cases in which discrepancies are identified. If a mismatch exceeds a certain tax threshold, AUR reviewers decide if it warrants a notice to the taxpayer asking for an explanation of the discrepancy or payment of any additional tax assessed. IRS guidance directs reviewers to consider the reasonableness of the taxpayers' responses, but reviewers generally do not examine the accuracy of the information in the responses because they do not have examination authority. For certain issues, AUR reviewers may refer cases for a correspondence examination.

Automated Substitute for Return Program:

The Automated Substitute for Return (ASFR) program uses data from the IRP system to identify persons who did not file returns, construct tax returns for certain nonfilers, and assess tax, interest, and penalties based on those substitute returns. IRS does not pursue all of the constructed returns. Potential cases fall into one of ten priority levels and are worked highest-priority first. ASFR officials said they make budget decisions by taking into account the resources available to the program and determine the level of new cases that will be worked over the following year. In fiscal year 2011, the ASFR program closed nearly 1.4 million cases.

Correspondence Examinations: Correspondence examinations are formal audits of individual taxpayers but do not involve face-to-face meetings with taxpayers. Instead, these examinations target specific issues that are limited in scope and complexity, easily documented, and can be handled quickly and efficiently through correspondence between the taxpayer and the IRS examiner. Tax returns are selected as potential cases through automated business rules that filter or select tax returns according to predetermined criteria. These business rules can detect multiple potential issues, all of which can be worked through a single correspondence exam. Examiners have the authority to review additional issues on a return even if they were not identified by the automatic filters.

Field Examinations: Field examinations are conducted in face-to-face meetings between the taxpayer and the IRS examiner. These audits are targeted at individual returns with broader and more complex issues. Unlike correspondence examinations, the field examination program has a classification process where an experienced tax examiner will review a potential case to determine which, if any, issues should be examined. Individual tax returns are selected for field examination in a variety of ways. Some returns are selected in the pursuit of specifically identified compliance issues, such as abusive transactions or offshore compliance. Others are selected on the basis of a statistical formula that attempts to predict the potential for additional tax assessments, and yet others are selected randomly for research purposes. Regardless of why the return was initially selected for audit, an examiner will review the return in its entirety to determine if other issues are present.

The responsibility for operating these individual taxpayer enforcement programs largely rests with IRS's Small Business/Self-Employed (SB/SE) Division, which handles complex individual returns, and Wage and Investment (W&I) Division, which handles simpler returns. SB/SE operates parts of all four IRP and exam programs; W&I operates parts of three programs, excluding field examinations.

Examinations of Taxpayers with Less than $200,000 in Positive Income Accounted for Most of the Total Cost of the Four Enforcement Programs

Most IRS Enforcement Resources are Spent on Examinations

Correspondence and field exams accounted for more than 80 percent of the total administrative costs of the four programs we reviewed over the 2-year period we examined. (Total costs include direct examination time, training and other offline activities of examiners, supervisory and administrative support, and other overhead costs allocable to each program.) Based on data for hourly costs and time spent on different types of cases that IRS provided, we estimated that the cost per case for field exams, $2,278, was many times greater than those for correspondence exams, $274, AUR, $52, and ASFR, $72. (See fig. 1.)

Figure 1: Cost Shares and Cost per Case for Four Exam and IRP Programs for Cases Opened in Fiscal Years 2007 and 2008

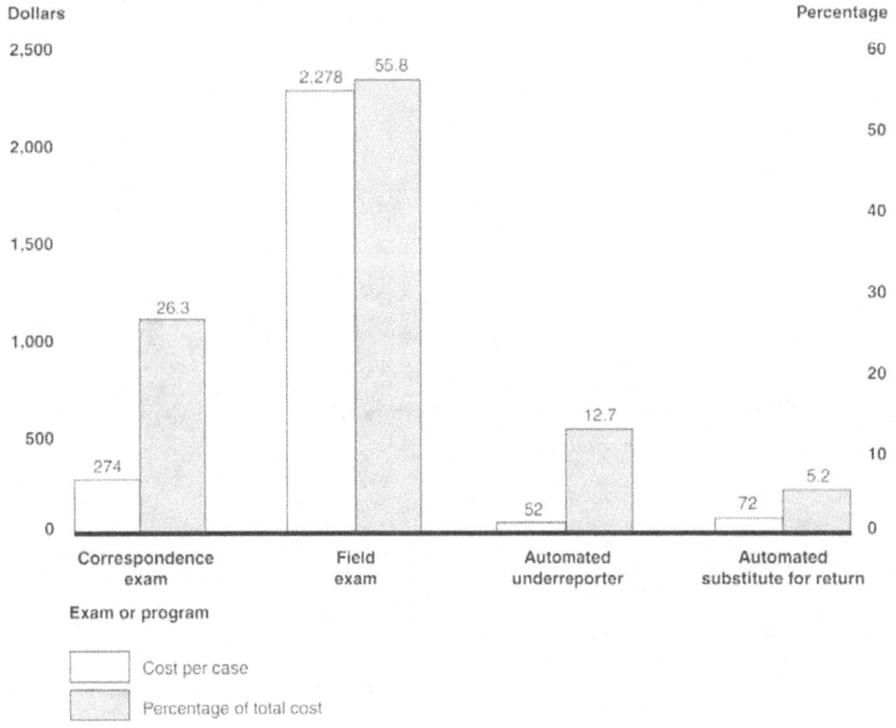

Source: GAO analysis of IRS data.

Note: Dollar figures have been adjusted for inflation to 2011 dollars using the GDP deflator.

High-Income Taxpayers Representing 3 Percent of Returns Filed Accounted for Almost 20 Percent of Total Exam Costs

IRS spent almost 20 percent of the $1.6 billion per year that it devoted to exams opened in 2007 and 2008 on returns with positive income of at least $200,000, even though such returns accounted for only 3 percent of the 136 million individual income tax returns filed per year.[5] The share of total cost for these returns was greater than their share of total returns because they were examined at above average rates and, compared to lower-income returns, field exams were a greater proportion of their examinations. (See fig. 2.)

[5]Exams opened in 2007 and 2008 were generally filed in 2006 and 2007.

Figure 2: Number of Returns, Exam Costs, and Coverage Rates for Different Categories of Individual Income Taxpayers

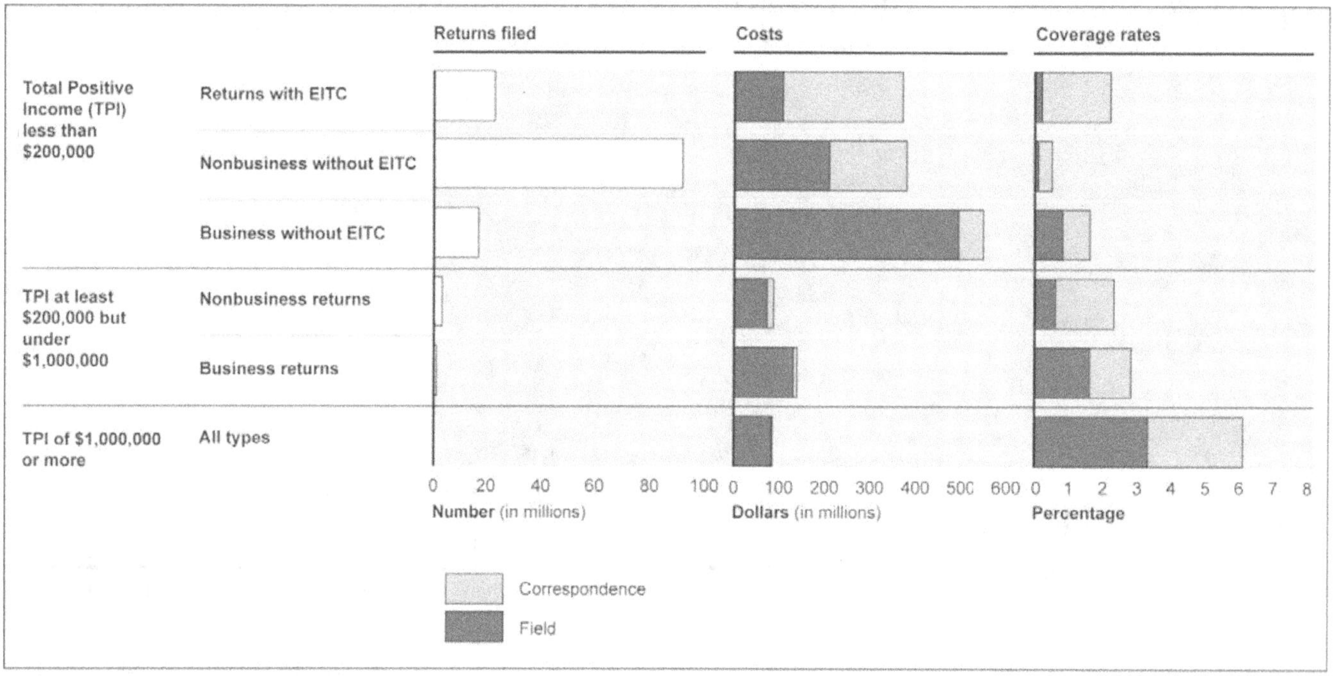

Source: GAO analysis of IRS data.

Note: Dollar figures have been adjusted for inflation to 2011 dollars using the GDP deflator.

Direct Revenue Return on Investment Was Highest for Examinations of Taxpayers with at Least $200,000 in Positive Income

For the 2 years of cases we reviewed, exams (both correspondence and field) of taxpayers with positive incomes of at least $200,000 produced significantly more direct revenue per dollar of cost than exams of lower-income taxpayers. Across income groups, correspondence exams were significantly more productive than field exams in terms of discounted direct revenue per dollar of cost. (See fig. 3 and table 1 in app. II.) We estimated that the average direct revenue yield per dollar of cost across all correspondence exams of individual taxpayers was $7. In contrast, the average direct yield per dollar for field exams of individual taxpayers was $1.8. We also estimated that the direct revenue per dollar of cost was about $22 for AUR cases and about $31 for ASFR cases.

Figure 3: Ratios of Direct Revenue to Costs for Different Types of Exams and Groups of Individual Income Tax Returns for Cases Opened in Fiscal Years 2007 and 2008

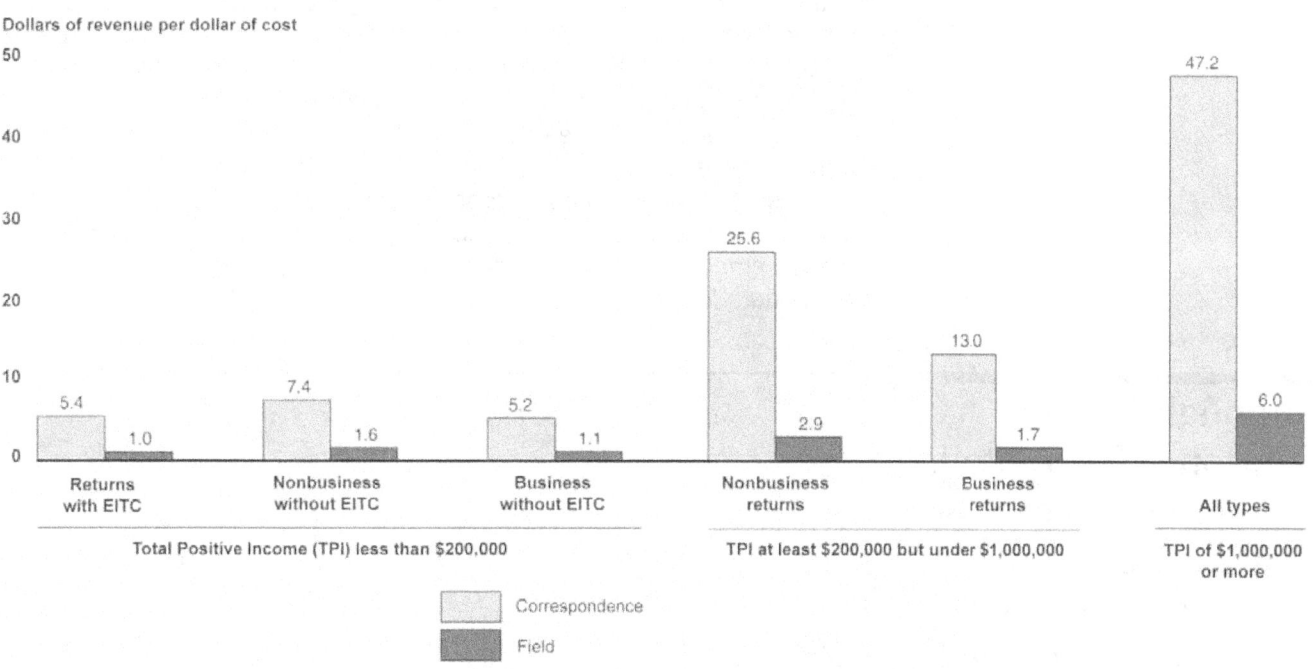

Dollars of revenue per dollar of cost

	Returns with EITC	Nonbusiness without EITC	Business without EITC	Nonbusiness returns	Business returns	All types
Correspondence	5.4	7.4	5.2	25.6	13.0	47.2
Field	1.0	1.6	1.1	2.9	1.7	6.0

Total Positive Income (TPI) less than $200,000 — TPI at least $200,000 but under $1,000,000 — TPI of $1,000,000 or more

Correspondence

Field

Source: GAO analysis of IRS data.

Note: Dollar figures have been adjusted for inflation to 2011 dollars using the GDP deflator. Direct revenue has been discounted over the gap between the year in which IRS incurred the exam costs and the year in which the revenue was collected.

Exams that are more complicated than average are likely to require both more time to complete and more highly skilled examiners, who cost more per hour. In estimating the results for field exams in figure 3, we incorporated differences in the amount of time spent on each field exam, which is recorded in the ERIS database, but we did not account for differences in hourly costs relating to varying skill levels of examiners across cases because the data available for that purpose were limited.[6] Nevertheless, to test the potential sensitivity of our results to this missing

---

[6]According to IRS officials, the ERIS data relating to time spent on correspondence exams are not reliable for our purposes. On their advice, given that neither the time spent on 1040 correspondence exams nor the skill level of examiners typically vary significantly from case to case, we used the same cost estimate for all cases, which IRS provided to us.

factor, we estimated an alternative set of field exam results, using an ERIS data element that reflects the expected difficulty of an exam. We also tested the effect of differences in locality pay for field examiners in different geographic locations. (See app. I for further details.) We found that adjusting for skill levels likely reduces some of the differences in direct revenue per dollar of cost across field exam categories; adjusting for location has a negligible effect. (See table 3 in app. II.) IRS would be able to estimate ratios of direct revenue to cost that better incorporate differences in the hourly costs across examiners with different skill levels if data from IRS's timekeeping system that records the number of hours that each employee charged to specific exam cases were matched to revenue data for the same cases.

Although Some Caution is Warranted, Exam Resource Reallocation Could Produce Significant Direct Revenue Gains

Modest Reallocations Might Raise Billions of Dollars in Direct Revenue with Little, If Any, Decline in Voluntary Compliance

Our analysis of a hypothetical reallocation of IRS examination resources for this 2-year period indicates that a shift of about $124 million in enforcement resources could have increased direct revenue by $1 billion over the $5.5 billion per year IRS actually collected. This result is based on shifting the $124 million from exams of lower-income returns with the earned income tax credit (EITC) and lower-income business returns without EITC to exams of higher-income returns and lower-income nonbusiness returns without EITC. The result holds true as long as the average ratio of direct revenue to cost for each category of returns remained unchanged.[7] (See fig. 4.) Similar gains would recur annually,

---

[7]The results presented in figure 4 and table 2 in appendix II are based on our estimates of direct revenue to cost from table 1. If, alternatively, we used the ratios for field exams that incorporate the adjustments for difficulty (from table 3) the direct revenue yield of our hypothetical reallocation would be about $900 million.

relative to the revenue that IRS otherwise would collect if it did not change its resource allocation and taxpayer behavior remained substantially the same.

Figure 4: Changes in Resources and Direct Revenue for Different Groups of Individual Income Tax Exams under a Hypothetical Reallocation

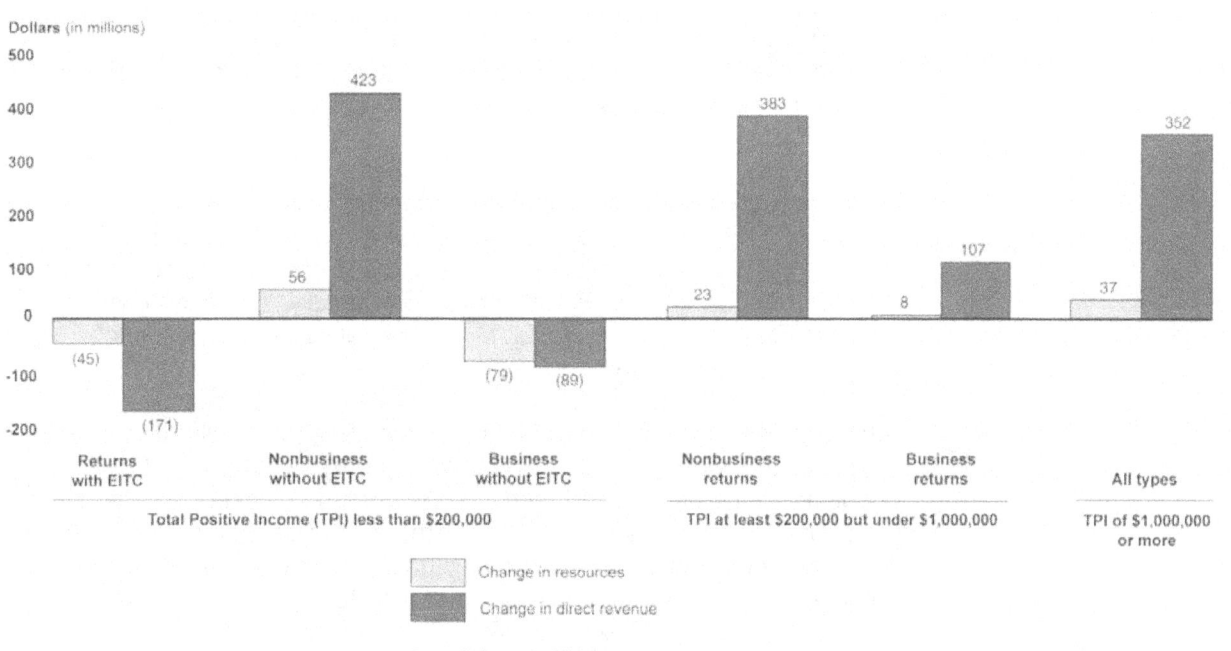

Source: GAO analysis of IRS data.

Notes: Negative amounts show resources taken away and corresponding revenue lost while positive amounts show increases. Dollar figures have been adjusted for inflation to 2011 dollars using the GDP deflator. Direct revenue has been discounted over the gap between the year in which IRS incurred the exam costs and the year in which the revenue was collected.

We took account of several constraints when designing our hypothetical resource reallocation example. First, we did not want to suggest a large-scale change because some reallocations cannot be made quickly, particularly if they require a different distribution of examiner skills than exists in IRS's current workforce. The $124 million that we shifted represents less than 8 percent of the $1.6 billion per year that IRS devoted to examinations of individual tax returns for the 2 years we studied and we shifted less than 5 percent of existing field exam resources ($1.1 billion per year) to correspondence exams.[8] Second, we did not want to end up with extreme coverage rates (either high or low) in any return category. Therefore, we did not reduce the combined coverage rate for any category for which the coverage rate was already close to or below 1 percent, and we kept the highest coverage rate (for returns with positive incomes of $1 million or more) under 11 percent.[9] (Nevertheless, that 11 percent rate is almost twice the current rate for that category.) Finally, given that certain compliance issues can be reviewed effectively only through a field exam, we did not decrease field exam resources in any return category for which we increased correspondence exam resources.

Exam resource reallocation can also affect tax collections indirectly by influencing the voluntary compliance of nonexamined taxpayers. These indirect effects are difficult to estimate and IRS has no empirical evidence that would allow it to say whether overall voluntary compliance would increase or decrease as a result of specific resource reallocations. Changes in exam coverage rates are generally believed to affect voluntary compliance by altering taxpayers' perceived risks of being audited. The higher the risk of being audited, the less inclined taxpayers are to evade taxes. As shown in figure 5, our hypothetical reallocation would have increased combined coverage rates in most of the tax return categories we examined. For those categories in which coverage rates declined, the declines were relatively modest. For these reasons we believe that the direct revenue gains associated with our hypothetical reallocation would not likely be offset by significant indirect revenue losses. However, if larger resource allocations were considered, the lack of empirical evidence on the potential changes in voluntary compliance could leave IRS uncertain of the extent to which direct revenue gains might be offset by negative indirect revenue effects. Although research on this issue is challenging, IRS might be able to leverage its existing efforts to study voluntary compliance through the National Research Program (NRP) to get better information on the influence of enforcement activity on voluntary compliance.

---

[8]See table 1 in appendix II for details of the existing allocation across groups and table 2 for details on the reallocations.

[9]The combined coverage rate equals the number of correspondence and field exams for a particular group, divided by the number of returns filed by that group.

Figure 5: Coverage Rates for Different Types of Exams and Groups of Individual Income Tax Returns Before and After Hypothetical Reallocation

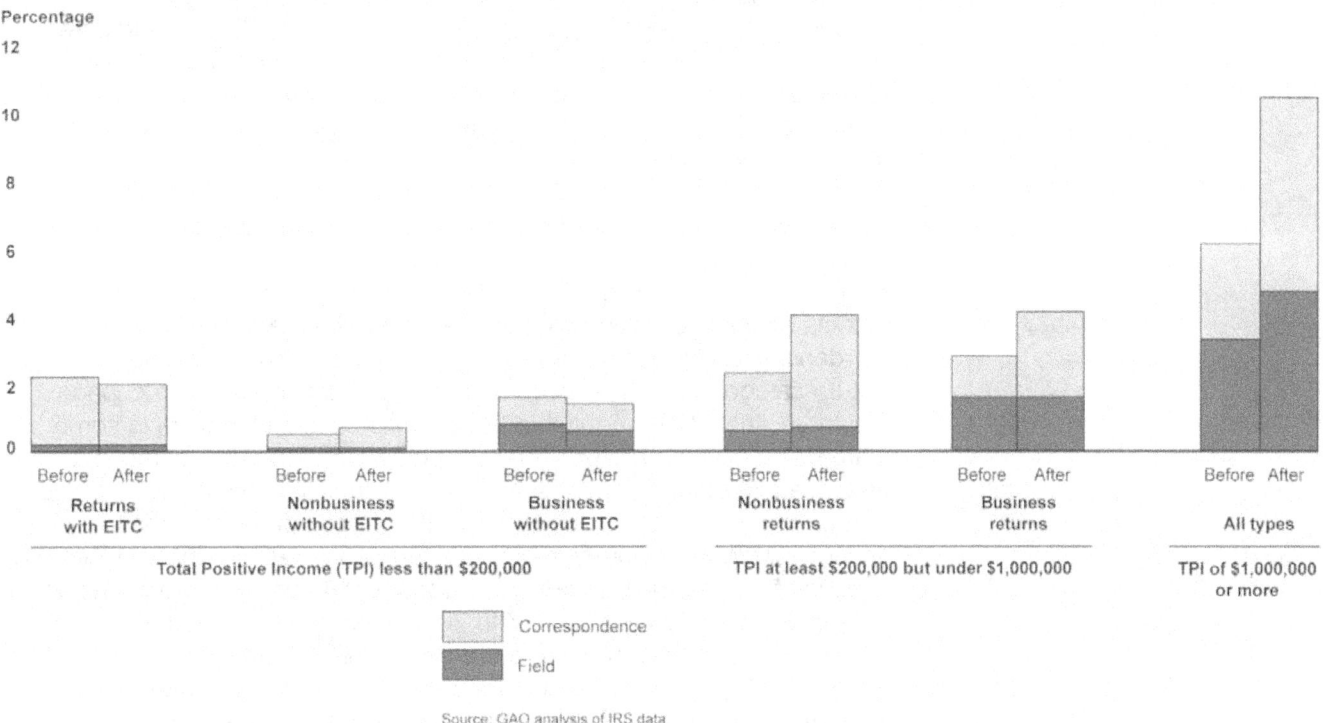

Source: GAO analysis of IRS data

Consideration of Additional Factors Could Improve Upon Allocation Decisions that are Based Solely on Ratios of Average Direct Revenue to Costs

Our analysis focused upon ratios of average direct revenue to average cost. We did not incorporate other potentially important considerations due to data constraints. One such consideration is the extent to which the ratio of direct revenue per dollar of cost may decline for a particular category of exams as additional resources are devoted to that category. The revenue yield of each additional return that IRS exams within a particular return category may be lower than the average revenue-productivity rates we estimated, particularly if IRS's return selection process for examinations results in returns with the greatest revenue potential being worked first and those with the least potential being worked last. Little is known about the relationship between marginal and average revenue and cost within specific return categories because IRS currently does not identify the marginal cases worked each year.[10] Until IRS collects some information on marginal cases, such as how the broad characteristics of those returns that would likely be selected (or not selected) in a modest program expansion (or contraction) would differ from the average return actually audited now, planners would have to rely solely upon ratios of average direct revenue to average cost—a less accurate basis for estimating the direct revenue consequences of specific exam resource allocations.

An analysis of the marginal revenue yields for specific categories of returns might also enable IRS to reduce the number of audits that result in no direct change in tax liability (although they may have beneficial effects on voluntary compliance). These no-change cases impose burdens on compliant taxpayers. Further, substantial variations across return categories in the percentage of exams that result in no change could be viewed as inequitable because compliant taxpayers in some categories have a greater chance of being burdened than compliant taxpayers in other categories. No-change rates in some higher-income return categories are already relatively high, compared to rates for lower-income categories. For example, the no-change rate for correspondence exams of tax returns with positive income of $1 million or more was about 53 percent for fiscal years 2007 to 2008. (See table 1 in app. II.) However, the highest no-change rates are associated with correspondence exams, which should be less burdensome than field exams. High no-change rates could also be associated with declining revenue yields in marginal cases; however, without a specific study of marginal cases, it is not possible to say whether no-change cases are concentrated among the last cases examined in a particular category or whether they are spread relatively evenly across exams worked throughout the course of the year.

---

[10]Marginal revenue and cost are those associated with the marginal cases worked in each return category. The marginal cases are those that would not have been worked if the resources allocated to a particular category had been slightly less, as well as those additional cases that would have been worked if the resources for the category had been slightly greater. Some of IRS's exam priorities are related to potential revenue yield; however, IRS also gives high priority to returns randomly selected for the National Research Program. This random selection process is important to the research that identifies significant areas of noncompliance, but it represents one reason to doubt that exam cases worked lower down the list of IRS's priorities always have lower returns than those worked earlier.

Factors other than revenue yields and IRS budget costs also matter for purposes of an overall cost-benefit evaluation of IRS exam activities. These activities impose compliance costs on taxpayers and economic efficiency costs on society. Return categories with low ratios of direct revenue to IRS budget costs could have offsetting advantages in terms of lower efficiency and compliance costs; however, no empirical evidence of variations in these other effects or costs across the return categories exists, nor would it be easy to obtain. (See app. III for further discussion of these tradeoffs.)

Conclusions

The results of our analyses suggest that there is potential for IRS to increase the direct revenue yield of selected enforcement programs by hundreds of millions of dollars per year without significant (if any) adverse effect on the indirect effect that examinations have on revenues. However, our results are preliminary and limited in scope. The collection and analysis of additional data would help to both confirm our basic conclusion and assist IRS in more finely adjusting its resource allocation decisions. One priority would be to study the feasibility of estimating the marginal revenue and marginal costs within each program within each taxpayer group. It would be helpful, for example, to estimate at least how the broad characteristics of those returns that would likely be selected (or not selected) in a modest program expansion (or contraction) would differ from the average return actually audited now. Such information would help IRS assess the extent to which revenue productivity would likely decline, if at all, if more exam resources are devoted to a particular group of taxpayers. Another useful project would be to see if some linkage could be made between the amounts of time that specific examiners spend on each case and the revenue collection amounts for each case that are recorded in ERIS. Such a link would enable IRS to estimate ratios of direct revenue to cost that better incorporate differences in the hourly costs across examiners with different skill levels. The collection or estimation of other information that would be useful when allocating resources, such as the influence of enforcement activity on voluntary compliance, is challenging, which is why little is known about those topics to date. Nevertheless, IRS might be able to leverage its existing efforts to study voluntary compliance through the NRP to get better information on the influence of enforcement activity on voluntary compliance.

In the absence of the additional data identified above, IRS planners can use the results of an analysis such as ours in combination with their professional judgment to decide whether the potential for direct revenue gains more than offsets the potential for reductions in indirect revenue or in equity and any increases in compliance or efficiency costs. If the answer is positive, they can adjust their allocation of resources accordingly. Nevertheless, the better empirical basis IRS planners have for making such judgments, the more confident they can be that they are allocating their limited resources to the best effect.

Recommendations

To better ensure that IRS's limited enforcement resources are allocated in a manner that maximizes the revenue yield of the income tax, subject to other important objectives of tax administration, such as minimizing compliance costs and ensuring equitable treatment across different groups of taxpayers, the Commissioner of Internal Revenue should:

- review disparities in the ratios of direct revenue yield to costs across different enforcement programs and across different groups of cases within programs and determine whether this evidence provides a basis for adjusting IRS's allocation of enforcement resources each year.

As part of this review, IRS should:

- develop estimates of the marginal direct revenue and marginal direct cost within each enforcement program and each taxpayer group;
- compile data on the amount of time that specific grades of examiners and downstream employees spend on specific categories of exams that can be identified in ERIS; and
- explore the potential of estimating the marginal influence of enforcement activity on voluntary compliance, potentially taking advantage of new NRP data.

Agency Comments

We requested written comments from the Commissioner of Internal Revenue and received a letter from IRS Deputy Commissioner for Services and Enforcement on November 29, 2012, (which is reprinted in app. IV). IRS agreed with our recommendations and agreed that the development of additional key data will require considerable work. In recognition of the time it will take to obtain this information, IRS said it will consider how to apply interim methods, findings, or approximations.

As agreed with your offices, unless you publicly announce the contents of this report earlier, we plan no further distribution until 30 days from the report date. At that time, we will send copies to interested congressional committees, the Secretary of the Treasury, the Commissioner of Internal

Revenue, and other interested parties. In addition, the report also will be available at no charge on the GAO website at http://www.gao.gov.

If you or your staff have any questions about this report, please contact me at (202) 512-9110 or whitej@gao.gov. Contact points for our Offices of Congressional Relations and Public Affairs may be found on the last page of this report. GAO staff who made major contributions to this report are listed in appendix V.

James R. White
Director, Tax Issues
Strategic Issues

Appendix I: Summary Methodology for Data Analysis

Our principal analysis compares the costs and direct revenues associated with correspondence and field exams that were opened during fiscal years 2007 and 2008 across the principal categories of individual taxpayers that the Internal Revenue Service (IRS) uses for exam planning purposes. These categories, defined in terms of income size and the nature of items reported on the returns, are shown in table 1 of appendix II.

Exam Costs

IRS provided us with total cost estimates for correspondence exams (with and without the earned income tax credit (EITC)) and field exams (with and without EITC) from its Integrated Financial System. These total cost estimates included all direct examiner costs, training and other off-line activities of examiners, supervisory and administrative support, and other overhead costs allocable to each program. We estimated hourly costs by dividing the total costs by the average examination hours per case, which IRS provided for correspondence exams (with and without the earned income tax credit (EITC)) and field exams (with and without EITC) from its Audit Information Management System (AIMS).[1] These hourly cost estimates are adequate for the relatively high-level comparisons we present in this report. IRS would be able to make more precise estimates for more detailed categories of exams if data from IRS's timekeeping system that records the number of hours that each employee charged to specific exam cases were matched to revenue data for the same cases.

To estimate the cost for each category of field exams we multiplied the hourly cost rates by the number of direct hours reported in the Enforcement Revenue Information System (ERIS) for each category of exam.[2] According to IRS officials the ERIS data relating to time spent on correspondence exams is not reliable for our purposes.[3] On their advice, given that neither the time spent on 1040 correspondence exams nor the

---

[1] IRS provided six separate estimates for the total costs and the average examination hours per case—for Wage and Investment correspondence exams of returns with and without EITC, for Small Business/Self-Employed (SB/SE) correspondence exams of returns with and without EITC, and for SB/SE field exams of returns with and without EITC.

[2] ERIS examination hours data originate in AIMS.

[3] We determined that ERIS data were sufficiently reliable for other purposes identified in this report.

skill level of examiners typically vary significantly from case to case, we used the same cost estimate for all cases, which IRS provided to us. We restated the costs for each case in terms of 2011 dollars by adjusting for inflation. Due to limitations of the ERIS data our cost estimates do not include any downstream costs that IRS's Collections function may have devoted to these cases or any costs associated with examinations of pass-through entities that could have improved the productivity of some of these 1040 exams. We do not know whether the prevalence of these missing costs varies significantly across our exam categories; however, we do note that the one category we studied that specifically excluded returns with pass-through income had ratios of revenue to costs that were greater or equal to the ratios for the one category identified as likely to include such returns.[4]

Direct Revenues

We aggregated all of the tax, interest, and penalty collections recorded in ERIS for the same fiscal years, exam types, and taxpayer categories used for the cost side of our analysis. We also included amounts of refunds disallowed due to examinations in our definition of revenues. These amounts represent revenue saved for the government, even though IRS does not have to collect it after the exams.[5] We compiled the revenue data for each fiscal year in which the collections were made (through the end of fiscal year 2011) and restated the revenue in terms of 2011 dollars by adjusting for inflation.[6] Then we discounted the value of collections over the gap between the fiscal year in which IRS incurred the exam costs (which we estimated as being the midpoint of the exam) and the fiscal year in which the revenue was collected. The purpose of this discounting, which is standard practice for cost-benefit analyses, is to

---

[4]Returns without schedules C, E, F, or form 2106 contain no pass-through income; returns with schedule E or form 2106 are the most likely to include such income.

[5]One type of revenue savings that we could not include in our analysis due to data limitations was that associated with disallowances of loss or credit carry forwards. Additionally, corrections that IRS examiners make in taxpayers' favor should also be counted as social benefits arising from the exams because they improve the fairness of the tax system's application; however, such corrections were not identifiable in IRS's databases.

[6]Additional collections from these 2007 and 2008 cases could continue to come in after 2011, which implies that our ratios of revenue to cost may be slightly understated; however, the vast majority of collections typically are made within two years of exam closures.

account for the time-value of money between the time at which the government bears the cost of an activity or investment and the time at which it receives the related benefit. (We used a real discount rate for this discounting because we had already adjusted all of our figures for inflation.)

Incorporating Exam Difficulty and Location

The first set of estimates that we present in this report do not reflect potential differences in costs across exams due to the degree of experience demanded of the examiner or the location at which the exam was conducted. For a second set of estimates we adjusted the cost of field exams for relative difficulty. To do this we used ERIS data on hours by grade to compute a weighted average pay rate for all exams (for each combination of EITC and non-EITC and field or correspondence for each year). We then adjusted costs for each record by multiplying the cost by the mid-point pay rate for the grade of the record, divided by the weighted average difficulty pay rate for the relevant year and EITC status. For a third set of estimates we made this difficulty adjustment for field exams and then we also adjusted the costs of both correspondence and field exams for location differences by using data on the location of exams, hours, and locality pay for each location to compute a national average locality pay rate (weighted by the number of hours in each location) for each combination of field and correspondence exams of returns with and without EITC and a locality pay rate for each location. We then multiplied the cost estimate for each exam by the ratio of the national rate over the relevant location-specific rate.

Effects of a Hypothetical Resource Reallocation

The columns labeled "Change in Resources" in table 2 of appendix II show the amounts of IRS budget resources we moved out of or into specified exam categories for our hypothetical reallocation. These shifts were guided by the considerations we noted earlier. We estimated the revenue effect of each shift by multiplying the gain or loss of resources for each category by our estimated ratios of direct revenue to cost for those categories. We estimated the effect on the coverage rate within each category by multiplying the coverage rate prior to the reallocation by the percentage change in each category's resources caused by the reallocation.

Appendix II: Detailed Tables

Table 1: Costs, Direct Revenue, Exam Coverage Rates and No-Change Rates for Different Types and Groups of Exams Opened In Fiscal Years 2007 and 2008 (Weighted Average of the 2 Years)

Taxpayer group	Correspondence exams				Field exams				Combined coverage rate
	Cost per year ($ millions)	Direct revenue / cost	Coverage rate	No-change rate	Cost per year ($ millions)	Direct revenue / cost	Coverage rate	No-change rate	
Individual income tax returns, total	516.4	7.0	0.8%	15.5%	1,093.7	1.8	0.2%	11.5%	1.0%
Returns with total positive income under $200,000:									
Business and nonbusiness returns with earned income tax credit by size of total gross receipts:									
Under $25,000	247.5	5.5	1.8%	11.1%	22.9	1.2	0.1%	13.0%	1.9%
$25,000 or more	15.6	3.2	4.4%	11.1%	84.2	1.0	2.1%	8.5%	6.5%
Nonbusiness returns without earned income tax credit									
Without Schedules C, E, F, or Form 2106	114.4	7.9	0.4%	21.0%	89.8	1.6	0.1%	15.5%	0.4%
With Schedule E or Form 2106	56.2	6.5	0.9%	10.5%	119.1	1.6	0.3%	7.0%	1.3%
Business returns without earned income tax credit:									
Nonfarm business returns by size of total gross receipts:									
Under $25,000	32.9	5.7	0.8%	16.0%	128.3	1.2	0.5%	7.5%	1.2%
$25,000 under $100,000	13.8	4.4	1.0%	13.0%	98.7	1.0	1.0%	9.5%	1.9%
$100,000 under $200,000	8.2	5.5	2.2%	9.6%	95.6	1.2	2.8%	8.0%	5.0%
$200,000 or more	1.0	2.6	0.3%	45.1%	152.4	1.0	2.2%	15.4%	2.5%
Farm returns	1.0	3.5	0.2%	40.1%	17.6	2.0	0.2%	16.6%	0.5%
Returns with total positive income of at least $200,000 and under $1 million:									
Nonbusiness returns	14.6	25.6	1.7%	34.9%	72.3	2.9	0.6%	15.9%	2.3%
Business returns	8.2	13.0	1.2%	34.6%	130.9	1.7	1.6%	17.8%	2.9%
Returns with total positive income of $1 million or more	3.1	47.2	2.8%	52.7%	81.8	6.0	3.3%	21.3%	6.2%

Source: GAO analysis of IRS data.

Note: Dollar figures have been adjusted for inflation to 2011 dollars using the GDP deflator. Direct revenue has been discounted over the gap between the year in which IRS incurred the exam costs and the year in which the revenue was collected.

Table 2: Potential Changes in Direct Revenue and Exam Coverage Rates Resulting from a Hypothetical Reallocation of Exam Resources

Taxpayer group	Correspondence exams				Field exams			
	Change in resources ($ millions)	Change in direct revenue ($ millions)	Coverage rate before	Coverage rate after	Change in resources ($ millions)	Change in direct revenue ($ millions)	Coverage rate before	Coverage rate after
Individual income tax returns, total (net)	50.0	874.0			-50.0	130.1		
Returns with total positive income under $200,000:								
Business and nonbusiness returns with earned income tax credit by size of total gross receipts:								
Under $25,000	-26.4	-145.5	1.8%	1.6%				
$25,000 or more	-3.5	-11.3	4.4%	3.4%	-14.9	-14.1	2.1%	1.8%
Nonbusiness returns without earned income tax credit:								
Without Schedules C, E, F, or Form 2106	41.5	328.4	0.4%	0.5%				
With Schedule E or Form 2106	14.7	94.9	0.9%	1.2%				
Business returns without earned income tax credit:								
Nonfarm business returns by size of total gross receipts:								
Under $25,000								
$25,000 under $100,000	-1.7	-7.4	1.0%	0.9%	-26.5	-25.4	1.0%	0.7%
$100,000 under $200,000					-22.3	-26.8	2.8%	2.1%
$200,000 or more					-28.9	-29.4	2.2%	1.8%
Farm returns								
Returns with total positive income of at least $200,000 and under $1 million:								
Nonbusiness returns	14.0	356.7	1.7%	3.3%	9.1	26.5	0.6%	0.7%
Business returns	8.2	106.8	1.2%	2.5%				

Taxpayer group	Correspondence exams				Field exams			
	Change in resources ($ millions)	Change in direct revenue ($ millions)	Coverage rate before	Coverage rate after	Change in resources ($ millions)	Change in direct revenue ($ millions)	Coverage rate before	Coverage rate after
Returns with TPI of $1 million or more	3.2	151.4	2.8%	5.7%	33.6	200.2	3.3%	4.7%

Source: GAO analysis of IRS data.

Note: Dollar figures have been adjusted for inflation to 2011 dollars using the GDP deflator. Direct revenue has been discounted over the gap between the year in which IRS incurred the exam costs and the year in which the revenue was collected.

Table 3: Ratios of Direct Revenue to Cost for Field Exams Opened in 2007 and 2008 after Accounting for Various Factors

Taxpayer group	Adjusted for inflation and discounting	Adjusted for inflation, discounting and difficulty	Adjusted for inflation, discounting, difficulty and location
Individual income tax returns, total	1.8	1.8	1.8
Returns with total positive income under $200,000:			
Business and nonbusiness returns with earned income tax credit by size of total gross receipts:			
Under $25,000	1.2	1.2	1.2
$25,000 or more	1.0	1.0	1.0
Nonbusiness returns without earned income tax credit:			
Without Schedules C, E, F, or Form 2106	1.6	1.7	1.7
With Schedule E or Form 2106	1.6	1.8	1.8
Business returns without earned income tax credit:			
Nonfarm business returns by size of total gross receipts:			
Under $25,000	1.2	1.3	1.3
$25,000 under $100,000	1.0	1.0	1.0
$100,000 under $200,000	1.2	1.2	1.2
$200,000 or more	1.0	1.0	1.0
Farm returns	2.0	1.8	1.9
Returns with total positive income of at least $200,000 and under $1 million:			
Nonbusiness returns	2.9	2.7	2.7
Business returns	1.7	1.6	1.6
Returns with TPI of $1 million or more	6.0	5.1	5.0

Source: GAO analysis of IRS data.

Note: Dollar figures have been adjusted for inflation to 2011 dollars using the GDP deflator. Direct revenue has been discounted over the gap between the year in which IRS incurred the exam costs and the year in which the revenue was collected.

Appendix III: Economic Guidelines for Enforcement Resource Allocation Decisions

An economic cost-benefit evaluation of IRS's overall activities would involve a comparison of the social costs and social benefits associated with those activities.[1] IRS's function is to collect tax revenue that the federal government transfers among citizens as cash payments or in the form of goods and services. The collection process imposes costs on society but produces no direct benefit itself. The government's use of the collected revenue may ultimately produce a net benefit for society if the social value of that use exceeds the social cost of raising the revenue. IRS has no influence over how tax revenue is used; it can only contribute to increasing the net social benefit by increasing the amount of revenue collected for a given amount of social cost (or decreasing the social cost of raising a given amount of revenue). Specific resource allocation choices can be compared on the basis of the amount of revenue they produce for a given amount of total social costs.

Components of Total Social Costs

The social costs of tax collection comprise the following:

- IRS budget costs.
- Tax burden. This is the actual money collected from taxpayers. Amounts collected as a result of IRS enforcement activities from taxpayers who, otherwise, would have been noncompliant may have a zero social cost. The cost that those amounts represent can be attributed to the tax law, rather than to IRS enforcement efforts. If those additional amounts of taxes due are not collected, the tax burdens evaded by noncompliant individuals are offset by the additional taxes that compliant taxpayers must pay in order to support a given government budget.
- Compliance burden. IRS's enforcement activities can affect the costs that taxpayers incur when complying with the tax law by increasing the time and money that they spend preparing their returns and interacting with IRS.

[1]Social costs are the sum of all private costs and any external costs to society arising from the production of a good or service. Private costs are incurred by producers of goods and services and are reflected in the prices charged to consumers for those goods and services. External costs are costs arising from production, such as pollution, that are borne by third parties (other than the producers or consumers). Similarly, social benefits are the sum of all private benefits and any external benefits arising from the production of a good or service.

- Efficiency costs. IRS's enforcement activities can alter the tax avoidance and evasion behavior of individuals, which affects the efficiency of resource allocation in the economy. If an enforcement activity increases the aggregate costs of tax avoidance and evasion, economic efficiency and the average standard of living is reduced. Conversely, if the activity reduces such aggregate costs, economic efficiency would improve.
- Equity costs. IRS's resource allocation can affect how exam-related compliance burdens are distributed across different groups of taxpayers and also how the risk of noncompliant taxpayers getting penalized for evasion varies across groups. It is difficult to know what society as a whole would view as an equitable distribution of these burdens and risks; therefore it is difficult to assess the equity effects of any particular reallocation of resources.

The only component of social costs that can be reliably measured is the IRS budget cost, and it is difficult to attribute even that cost to very specific enforcement activities (such as specific audits). Consequently, IRS planners cannot consider all types of social costs in a rigorously quantitative manner when making their resource allocation decisions.

Marginal Analysis

Economists use the term "margin" when referring to the scopes of the various types of decisions that individuals make. For example, if IRS examination planners were deciding how to allocate the last million dollars of their budget between different types of audits, the marginal social cost of the choice they made would be a million dollars, plus the sum of all other social costs resulting from the IRS activities supported by that million dollars. The marginal revenue would be the amount of additional tax collections attributable (both directly and indirectly) to those activities. The most economically efficient choice would be the one that produced the highest ratio of marginal revenue to marginal social cost.

The ratio of marginal revenue to marginal social cost provides a basis for comparing the cost of collecting taxes by different approaches. Such comparisons can be made across broadly defined approaches (e.g., increasing taxpayer services to promote higher voluntary compliance versus increasing enforcement efforts to reduce noncompliance). Alternatively, as in this study, comparisons could be made across more narrowly defined alternatives (e.g., devoting more resources to audits of taxpayers with incomes below a certain amount versus devoting those resources to audits of taxpayers with incomes above that amount).

Appendix IV: Comments from the Internal Revenue Service

DEPARTMENT OF THE TREASURY
INTERNAL REVENUE SERVICE
WASHINGTON, D.C. 20224

DEPUTY COMMISSIONER

November 29, 2012

Mr. James R. White
Director, Tax Issues
Strategic Issues Team
U.S. States Government Accountability Office
Washington, DC 20548

Dear Mr. White:

Thank you for the opportunity to review your draft report entitled, "Tax Gap: IRS Could Significantly Increase Revenues by Better Targeting Enforcement Resources" GAO-13-151.

The IRS is committed to the optimal allocation of our enforcement resources; that is why we select workload strategically. It is also why we account for factors other than just direct return on investment when allocating resources across programs or categories of work.

As you noted in the report, there are two important shortcomings to using average direct revenue-to-cost ratios as the basis for resource allocation: (1) overall net revenue is maximized by equalizing the *marginal* (rather than average) ratio of revenue to cost across all relevant activities; and (2) the revenue reflected in those ratios must also include the *indirect* impact of our activities on the voluntary compliance of the taxpayers we contact as well as among others in the general population. Although we have made some headway in quantifying those two factors, these are very difficult things to estimate.

While we agree with your recommendation in principle, developing meaningful estimates of marginal and indirect effects remains a challenge as it will require improved data systems and new estimation techniques. These will take years to implement, not months. Until we implement the improved data systems and estimation techniques, we will not have an acceptable empirical basis for making perfect judgments about the disparities between average direct ratios of revenue to cost across enforcement activities. We will consider how we might apply interim methods, findings, or approximations as we pursue our research.

2

Again, I thank you for raising these important issues. If you have questions, please contact me, or a member of your staff may contact Pat McGuire, Deputy Director, Office of Research, Analysis and Statistics at (202) 927-5644.

Sincerely,

Steven T. Miller
Deputy Commissioner, Services and
Enforcement

Appendix V: GAO Contact and Staff Acknowledgments

GAO Contact	James R. White, (202) 512-9110 or whitej@gao.gov
Staff Acknowledgments	In addition to the contact named above, James Wozny (Assistant Director), Kevin Daly (Assistant Director), Michael Brostek, Ethan Wozniak, Suzanne Heimbach, Sara Daleski, Lois Hanshaw, Karen O'Conor, Ray Bush, Elizabeth Fan, and Robert MacKay made key contributions to this report.

GAO's Mission	The Government Accountability Office, the audit, evaluation, and investigative arm of Congress, exists to support Congress in meeting its constitutional responsibilities and to help improve the performance and accountability of the federal government for the American people. GAO examines the use of public funds; evaluates federal programs and policies; and provides analyses, recommendations, and other assistance to help Congress make informed oversight, policy, and funding decisions. GAO's commitment to good government is reflected in its core values of accountability, integrity, and reliability.
Obtaining Copies of GAO Reports and Testimony	The fastest and easiest way to obtain copies of GAO documents at no cost is through GAO's website (http://www.gao.gov). Each weekday afternoon, GAO posts on its website newly released reports, testimony, and correspondence. To have GAO e-mail you a list of newly posted products, go to http://www.gao.gov and select "E-mail Updates."
Order by Phone	The price of each GAO publication reflects GAO's actual cost of production and distribution and depends on the number of pages in the publication and whether the publication is printed in color or black and white. Pricing and ordering information is posted on GAO's website, http://www.gao.gov/ordering.htm. Place orders by calling (202) 512-6000, toll free (866) 801-7077, or TDD (202) 512-2537. Orders may be paid for using American Express, Discover Card, MasterCard, Visa, check, or money order. Call for additional information.
Connect with GAO	Connect with GAO on Facebook, Flickr, Twitter, and YouTube. Subscribe to our RSS Feeds or E-mail Updates. Listen to our Podcasts. Visit GAO on the web at www.gao.gov.
To Report Fraud, Waste, and Abuse in Federal Programs	Contact: Website: http://www.gao.gov/fraudnet/fraudnet.htm E-mail: fraudnet@gao.gov Automated answering system: (800) 424-5454 or (202) 512-7470
Congressional Relations	Katherine Siggerud, Managing Director, siggerudk@gao.gov, (202) 512-4400, U.S. Government Accountability Office, 441 G Street NW, Room 7125, Washington, DC 20548
Public Affairs	Chuck Young, Managing Director, youngc1@gao.gov, (202) 512-4800 U.S. Government Accountability Office, 441 G Street NW, Room 7149 Washington, DC 20548

www.ingramcontent.com/pod-product-compliance
Lightning Source LLC
Chambersburg PA
CBHW081242170526
45165CB00009B/3166